inquiring
INSPIRING
inclusive

Family Ministry
St. Mark's Episcopal Cathedral
519 Oak Grove Street
Minneapolis, MN 55403

Read @ CN 9/27/005

Dedicated to Kathy Bozzuti-Jones
and Mark Anthony Francisco Bozzuti-Jones II,
who teach me the blessings of God's creation.
—M. B. J.

To the congregation
at Bethany Lutheran Church
in Boone, North Carolina.
—S. H.

JESUS, THE WORD

Text copyright © 2005 Mark Bozzuti-Jones. Illustrations copyright © 2005 Shelly Hehenberger. All rights reserved. Except for brief quotations in critical articles or reviews, no part of this book may be reproduced in any manner without prior written permission from the publisher. Write to: Permissions, Augsburg Fortress, Publishers, P. O. Box 1209, Minneapolis, MN 55440-1209.

Large-quantity purchases or custom editions of this book are available at a discount from the publisher. For more information, contact the sales department at Augsburg Fortress, Publishers, 800-328-4648, or write to: Sales Director, Augsburg Fortress, Publishers, P. O. Box 1209, Minneapolis, MN 55440-1209.

ISBN 0-8066-5169-5

Cover and book design by Michelle L. N. Cook

The paper used in this publication meets the minimum requirements of American National Standard for Information Sciences—Permanence of Paper for Printed Library Materials, ANSI Z329.48-1984. ♾ ™

Manufactured in Singapore

09   08   07   06   05   1   2   3   4   5   6   7   8   9   10

In the beginning was the Word,
and the Word was with God,
and the Word was God.
All things came into being through him,
and without him not one thing came into being.
What has come into being in him was life . . .
and the Word became flesh
and lived among us,
and we have seen his glory.
—*John 1:1-4, 14*

In the beginning,
before everything,
the Word lived.

The Word was Love,
the Word was God,
God's Love, God's Word.

In the beginning,
the Word created

heaven and earth

light and dark

sun and moon

oceans and rivers

rocks and hills

trees and flowers

animals of all kinds

and all people . . .

people just like

you and me.

In the beginning,

the Word was seen and unseen

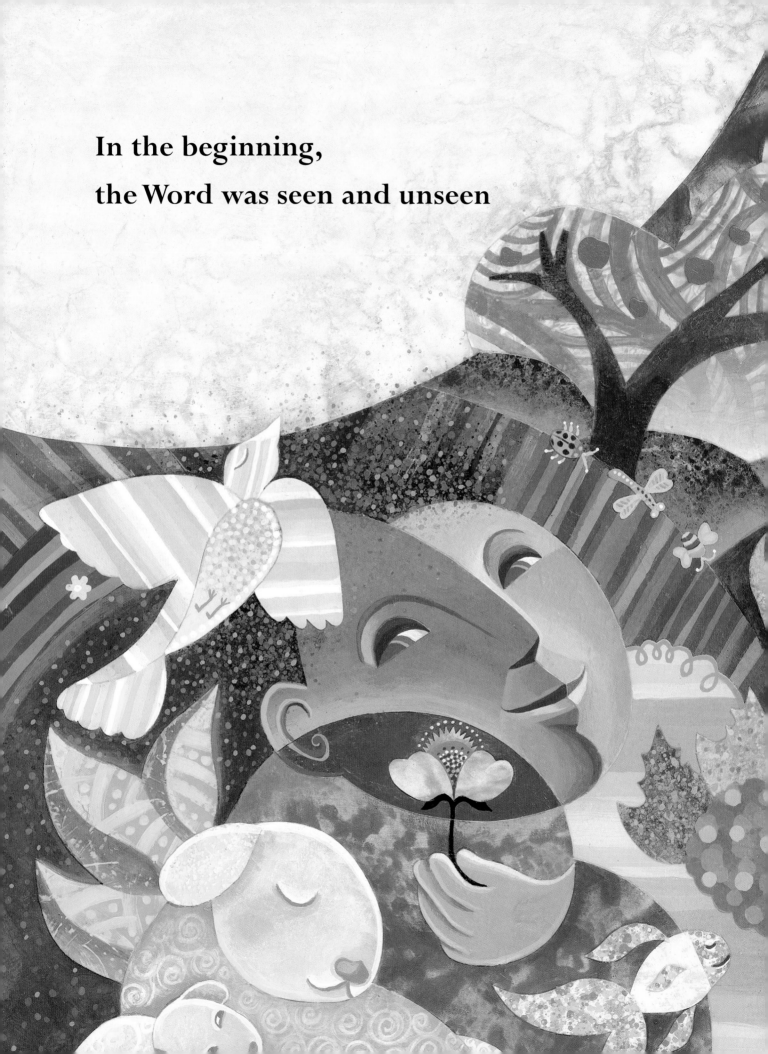

light for all eyes
sound for all ears
scent for all noses
food for all bodies
warmth for all creation

one with all things.

The Word came to earth.

God's Word was spoken . . .

spoken on mountain tops
spoken in the desert
spoken on the seas.

All of creation
whispered and echoed
the Word of God.

The Word of God said:

I will set you free.

I won't let you be anything

but holy, good, and free.

The Word spoke through the ages

for all people . . .

just like you and me.

The Word came down from heaven.
By the power of the Holy Spirit,
he became a child
born of a woman named Mary.

The Word was Jesus!

Jesus, the Word,
living among us and with us

mending broken hearts
wiping tears from crying eyes
feeding the poor with bread and hope.

Jesus, the Word,
living among us and with us

healing the blind and sick
making the lame walk
speaking God's love to all people.

Jesus, the Word, said:

I will set you free.
I won't let you be anything
but holy, good, and free.

The Word spoke
through the ages
for all people . . .

just like you and me.

But some people
turned their backs on Jesus, the Word.

They did not listen.

They did not believe in him.
They judged him.

They nailed him to a tree.

Jesus, the Word,
died
and was buried.

**But on the third day,
Jesus, the Word, rose from the dead.**

**God's Word spoke again:
"Do not be afraid."**

"Peace be with you."

Then Jesus, the Word, went up to heaven.

But the Word did not leave us.
Even today, the Word of God

forgives us

saves us

blesses us

fills us with the Holy Spirit.

God's Love lives within us.

The Word of God says: I will set you free.
I won't let you be anything
but holy, good, and free.

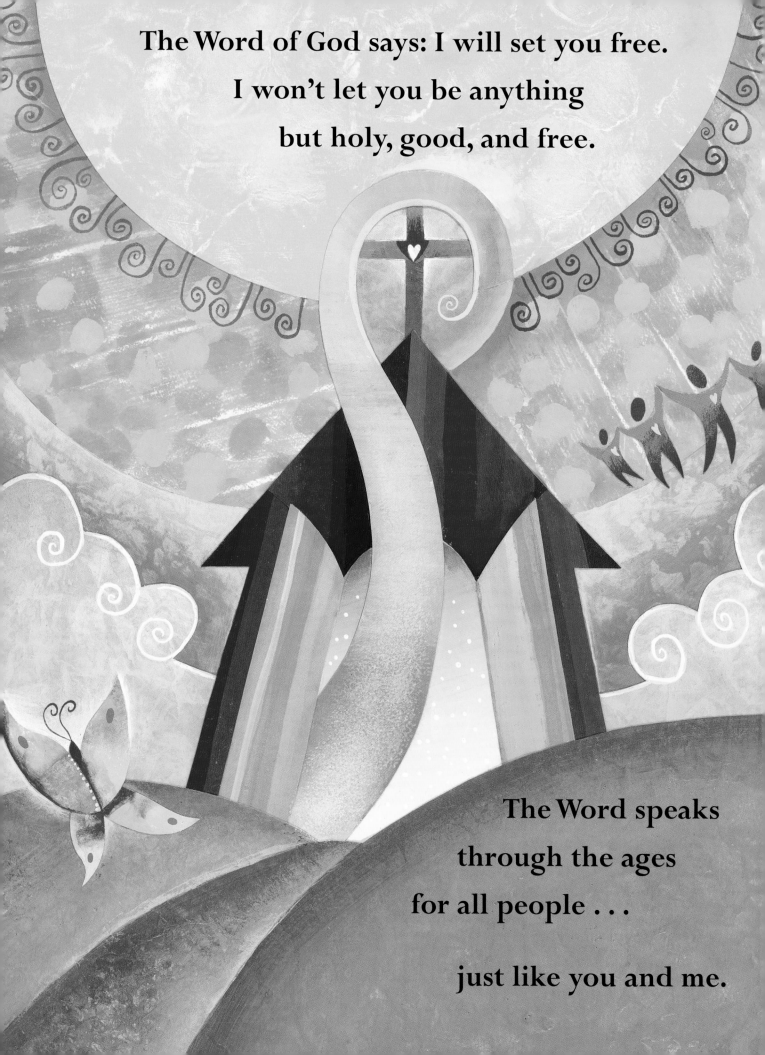

The Word speaks
through the ages
for all people . . .

just like you and me.